THE THIRD WAY

A 14-DAY MISSION PILGRIMAGE PRAYER JOURNAL

CHRIS SURBER

Energion Publications
Gonzalez, Florida
2017

ISBN10: 1-63199-465-4
ISBN13: 978-1-63199-465-4

Energion Publications
P. O. Box 841
Gonzalez, FL 32560

energion.com
pubs@energion.com

FOREWORD

It's difficult to be a pilgrim in a consumer world. A pilgrim is someone who looks more toward the destination than his present place. A consumer sets up shop as he secures more to consume and invests his time, resources, and energy into guaranteeing there will always be more to consume. In Luke 17:33 Jesus says, "If you cling to your life, you will lose it, and if you let your life go, you will save it."

I have no doubt that you'll make some important contributions to the community in which we are going to serve. I'm equally convinced that your contributions will pale in comparison to what God is about to do in your life. This is a pilgrimage of faith. We need to become pilgrims in a world of settlers.

It's difficult to be distinctly Christian in a world that is always pulling for our affections. In our culture, people define themselves as liberal or conservative, progressive or traditional. In Christ, we are merely defined as saved by grace and led by the Holy Spirit to the glory of God alone. In Luke 9:23 Jesus says, "If any of you wants to be My follower, you must turn from your selfish ways, take up your cross daily, and follow Me." That is the second principle this book is built around.

Among the joys of life on the mission field is discovering our identity rooted manifestly in Christ. When we get out of our daily trappings to serve God on a mission in a foreign land, we create the space necessary for our hearts to learn and relearn what it means to be simply His. We need to become decidedly Christian in a distracted world.

The Third Way is the way of Jesus. Not left. Not right. The Third Way is following Jesus in simplicity – finding our identity in Him alone! May God bless you on this journey!

Pastor Chris

TABLE OF CONTENTS

Week 1: Discovering Our Identity in Christ   Day 1

FINDING PEACE WITH GOD

"This means that anyone who belongs to Christ has become a new person. The old life is gone; a new life has begun!" (2 Corinthians 5:17)

It's time to prepare for your upcoming mission trip. Get your clothes and snacks packed. Make sure that you're all caught up at home and somebody is prepared to feed and walk Fido and change Fluffy's litter box. Those kinds of things matter, but not as much as preparing your heart.

I have peace with God because...

"Look at the lilies and how they grow. They don't work or make their clothing, yet Solomon in all his glory was not dressed as beautifully as they are. And if God cares so wonderfully for flowers that are here today and thrown into the fire tomorrow, He will certainly care for you. Why do you have so little faith?" (Luke 12:27-28)

I practice peace with God in ...

Fluffy will survive a week without you. The food on your pilgrimage may be different than what you're used to, but God will provide for you. It's time to set concern over clothing, food, and our immediate responsibilities to the side and begin to enter more completely into our relationship with our Lord and His ability to use us in His service.

You may have grown up in Church. You may have seriously followed Jesus for a long time. You may even be new to Church and Jesus stuff. Wherever you are on the

The door to the storehouse of peace is always opened when faith turns the key.

1

journey of the with-God-life, a mission trip is an opportunity for a pilgrimage of service.

It's time to consider what it means to have peace with God and to trust Him. In the thought box above, complete the sentences with one or two words of your own. Below, take the time to journal, write a prayer, or jot down a few thoughts or experiences of your own connected to finding, having, and experiencing the peace of God in your personal life and in your life of Christian service.

> "I am leaving you with a gift–peace of mind and heart. And the peace I give is a gift the world cannot give. So don't be troubled or afraid." (John 14:27)

A THANKFUL HEART

"My old self has been crucified with Christ. It is no longer I who live, but Christ lives in me. So I live in this earthly body by trusting in the Son of God, who loved me and gave Himself for me." (Galatians 2:20)

What does it mean to be thankful to God? Today believers are pressured by a pluralistic and secular society to conform. The collective pressure upon us today is far stronger than it was even a decade or two ago.

It's still relatively easy to be a Christian in our culture. What has become more difficult is to be distinctly Christian. In order to maintain passion for God, our identity in Christ must be secure. In order for that to occur, we must keep thankfulness for what God has done, is doing, and will do in us, central in our hearts and minds.

"Be thankful in all circumstances, for this is God's will for you who belong to Christ Jesus." (1 Thessalonians 5:18)

We can't control the world around us. We can't even always control the world within us. What we can do is decide daily to enter every situation with a spirit of thanksgiving to God.

In Christ, we are new creations! We are not the same! We can't go on living like defeated weaklings or overconfident

I am thankful for what God has done *for* me ...

I am thankful for what God has done *in* me ...

Nothing compels the heart more powerfully in the direction of God than thankfulness for His amazing grace.

bullies. God is calling us out of depression and fear, out of over-compensating and boasting, into a new life with Him through faith in His Son as we are empowered by the supernatural indwelling of the Holy Spirit!

Consider then write down some of the things Christ has done for you and in you that you are thankful for. From what has He set you free? In what ways can you see newness of life in Christ manifest in and through you? And if you've never trusted Him as both Savior and Lord – what better time could there be than right now?

"Praise the LORD! Give thanks to the LORD, for He is good! His faithful love endures forever." (Psalms 106:1)

The Joy of Obedience

> "For God has not given us a spirit of fear and timidity, but of power, love, and self-discipline." (2 Timothy 1:7)

What are you afraid of? What people will think? That you will fail? What people will think if you fail?! Over the years in life and ministry, I have found that a lot of people are hindered by fear.

In fact, were it not for fear I'm convinced that most Christians would do great things for God instead of just a few of us taking the risks necessarily associated with obedience to God. But what is it that separates those who are obedient to God no matter what the cost and those who are crippled by fear?

I would suggest to you today that it is all about identity. Many of the greatest athletes, for example, grow up and families where their sports in which they excel were a regular part of their life from early childhood. In the world of mixed martial arts names like Machado or Gracie are legendary.

These physical warriors are trained from early childhood in their art. The very fact of their last name instills fear in their opponents. These warriors know their identity. We are spiritual warriors and we are called sons and daughters of the Most High!

The Bible says that at the name of Jesus our enemies must flee! You and I need

I can still obey God in spite of...

I can apply more obedience in the areas of ...

Obedience is the only path to joy!

to grab a hold of our identity in Jesus Christ. There is joy available when God's people give themselves over fully to their identity in Jesus Christ. The purest joy is the consequence of obedience because it is the fruit of the Holy Spirit at work in us.

Let's stop living under a false identity today and commit ourselves to living lives as sons and daughters of the mighty King!

Following the Lord's Leading

"For we are God's masterpiece. He has created us anew in Christ Jesus, so we can do the good things He planned for us long ago." (Ephesians 2:10)

How do I know that God has a specific plan for you? Because His Word says so! Ephesians 2:20 tells us that God saves us entirely. Nothing we can do make us a "masterpiece." Can the canvas make of itself a beautiful painting? Of Course not!

Our lives are the canvases upon which God creates beautiful works of mercy and grace. But God doesn't stop there. He doesn't redeem sinners just to fix them up and put them in a celestial art gallery.

The mercy of God that saves us is the mercy of God that works through us. Before the foundation of the earth God created beautiful works for us to walk in as a response to His superabundant grace. That is a comforting thought when it comes to obedience.

If God mapped out our good works long before He even created any of us, why should we be afraid to obey Him in pursuing them? You see, our identity is in Christ and our work was long ago settled. That means that as followers of Jesus we have already been equipped with everything we need to obey God's leading.

God directs me in these ways...

I can be more attentive to His leading ...

He who would do great things for God must learn to hear from God.

"Their responsibility is to equip God's people to do His work and build up the church, the body of Christ." (Ephesians 4:12)

The "they" in Ephesians 4:12 are people like me, pastors and teachers. The work to be done is for all of us. What works are already accomplished, settled, in the mind of God, just waiting for you to engage and completed them?

Somewhere there is a shovel with your name it next to a foundation waiting to be dug for a glorious work of God. Get busy listening to God! Get busy digging!

CONVERSATIONS WITH GOD

"He came into the very world He created, but the world didn't recognize Him." (John 1:10)

Have you believed on the Lord Jesus Christ for salvation? Have you placed your faith in Him? Has God pulled you to Himself and saved you? Then rejoice! You are a child of God!

You know, sometimes I'm tired. Sometimes I'm just exhausted. When I'm really tired laying down in my bed in early evening, my kids come to assault me with words. They just want to spend time with me. But every now and then I'll say, "Give dad thirty minutes to calm his mind and I'll come see you in the living room."

I love my kids but I get overwhelmed with life and occasionally we need to reset and be at least mildly unavailable. God is never that way! He doesn't tire. He doesn't grow weary. He is always available to speak to and listen to His children.

"Have you never heard? Have you never understood? The LORD is the everlasting God, the Creator of all the earth. He never grows weak or weary. No one can measure the depths of His understanding." (Isaiah 40:28)

Run to God in prayer every day. As you prepare your heart to leave soon on this

My prayer life suffers when...

My prayer life grows when...

Prayer begins in man speaking. It is complete in hearing God's voice.

9

mission pilgrimage, stop everything you're doing, set aside every distraction, and get along with God.

Prayer is not a one-way string of petitions. It isn't just a child standing at her dad's bedroom door listing her demands for this, that, and the other thing. It is a conversation. We quiet our souls before our Heavenly Father and seek Him in words of petition, words of repetition of Scripture, and in silence as we wait to hear His voice speak to us as the leading of the soul by the Holy Spirit.

A life of prayer is a journey of discovery. Only those who engage in it can know its beauty because in knowing it, we know God.

Finding the Faith Necessary

"Yes, I am the vine; you are the branches. Those who remain in Me, and I in them, will produce much fruit. For apart from Me you can do nothing." (John 15:5)

"Remain in me" may be the most comforting words of Scripture. Remain in me. Stay in me. Don't go anywhere else because you don't have to. I'm all you need. On the other hand, "apart from me" may be the least comforting words of Scripture.

Jesus says that apart from Him we can do nothing. That is, we can do nothing pleasing to God that is consistent with God's will for us individually or collectively as God's people. As followers of Jesus, our entire identities are wrapped up in Christ.

When we set out to do God's will, and pursue Him and His plan, on His path, there is nothing we cannot do for Him!

"For I can do everything through Christ, who gives me strength." (Philippians 4:13)

Stop worrying if you packed enough snacks for your week-long mission pilgrimage. Unless you still haven't packed of course! Do your part. Pack your bags. Get your affairs in order. Clean Fluffy's litter box and be sure to turn off the oven.

Most of all, though, remain in Christ! Let's take a few minutes right now to quiet our souls before the Lord and ask Him

> **Faith is like...**
>
> **Faith is for...**
>
> Few people learn how much faith they have until they learn how much faith they need.

specifically for the faith necessary for the journey ahead of us. We don't know exactly what this pilgrimage will entail. God will have someone for us to serve. He will have someone for us to help.

The most important thing is that if we trust Him for it and if we are obedient in it, He will glorify Himself in us. Nothing is more humbling or more joyous than being authentically used by God. That will only happen if we choose right now to remain in Him.

LIFE ON THE WAY

"For He has rescued us from the kingdom of darkness and transferred us into the Kingdom of His dear Son, who purchased our freedom [with His blood] and forgave our sins." (Colossians 1:13-14)

One cold winter morning, while serving as Pastor of the First Congregational Church of Peru, Illinois, I found a pitiful stray cat literally half frozen to a patch of ice outside of my office door. I didn't want to take in the cat. In fact, I don't even really like cats but Fluffy – as he came to be called – was so pitiful that I couldn't help but help him.

The church secretary and I got him unstuck from the sidewalk and we took him in. He moved in with my family. The kids named him. But try as we may, he remained wild. He would hide under stairs and viciously attack our legs. He desperately needed to be brushed but would become violent if I attempted to groom.

After one particularly violent attack at me and the cat brush, I turned him over to a no-kill shelter and wished him best of luck. Fluffy never learned his new identity. He never learned his new name. Have we?

"So now you Gentiles are no longer strangers and foreigners. You are citizens

> **My identity in Christ means that I am...**

> **My identity in Christ means that I am no longer...**

> **Jesus crashed into our shadowy world to rescue us from darkness and make us children of light!**

along with all of God's holy people. You are members of God's family." (Ephesians 2:19)

In order to be a blessing to other team members, to the mission activity you're serving with this week, and to the people to whom we'll be ministering cross-culturally, we've got to recognize – right now – who we are in Christ. The time has come to come out from under the stairs as a family member, not hiding from the light and being defensive.

It has been said that a candle loses nothing by lighting another candle. The time to shed and share the light of Christ is now!

Week 2: Discovering Christ in our Journey   Day 1

MORE OF HIS WELCOME

"Then Jesus said to His disciples, "If any of you wants to be My follower, you must turn from your selfish ways, take up your cross, and follow Me." (Matthew 16:24)

You did it! You had the courage to get off the couch. Most of following Jesus is just having the willingness to choose the Cross over the couch. This week you're going to see things you've never seen before, do things you've never done before, and most of all, enter into the lives of new people.

We need more of His welcome in our hearts. Think of the way you've been welcomed by a people who are not your own. Consider the effort, time, and resources spent and sacrificed in order to welcome you to this foreign place.

How will God use you this week to extend the extravagant welcome of God into your life, even as these people have welcomed you into theirs. Sure, you're the visitor. You're the guest. But you've come to serve not to be served! You've come as an ambassador of all the Christians who made it possible for you to know Jesus, to mature in Christ, and even to come on this mission pilgrimage.

In Matthew 20:28 the words of Jesus are recorded saying, "For even the Son of Man came not to be served but to serve others and to give His life as a ransom for

I can extend an extravagant welcome by...

I can accept the welcome offered by others by...

I am most like Jesus when strangers are my brothers and my sisters.

15

many." You are here as a pilgrim ambassador of Jesus Christ and as a representative for the Body of Christ in our land! It's time to serve.

It's time – RIGHT NOW – to set aside preferences, fears, pride, ego, whining, and all the rest of it. It's time – RIGHT NOW – to go "all in" on this pilgrimage. Every time I travel a mission for Jesus, I learn new things about myself, about the culture and language, and about my Lord.

We got off the couch. Now let's pick up our Cross. Let's do this together, as a team, as fellow followers of Jesus Christ.

UNCONDITIONAL LOVE

> "For God called you to do good, even if it means suffering, just as Christ suffered for you. He is your example, and you must follow in His steps." (1 Peter 2:21)

Everybody wants to change the world or, at the very least, we all feel like we should want to change the world. Here's the thing ... We can't change the world and we need to stop trying to change the world. God doesn't call us to aim that high. He calls us to do what we can, where we are, with what we have.

Some people will do things for God that may seem big because they are publicized, written about, and memorialized. We see that and think we should mimic that. We're not called to solve the world's problems. The calling of every follower of Jesus is to mimic Jesus. That's it and that's enough.

God has showered us with the unconditional love of Jesus Christ. Jesus entered into our suffering, took part in it, and redeemed it! That's what God is calling us to do today. Right now.

Unconditional love necessarily includes suffering with others because that's what unconditional love is! Unconditional love says, "Your problems are my problems! This world is broken and I'm a little less broken than you today, so here's my pres-

Unconditional love does / is...
Unconditional love does not / is not...
Unconditional love is love without boundaries, borders, or limits.

ence in your pain! I'm with you! You're not alone! Jesus is with us both!"

God didn't bring you or me on this mission pilgrimage to solve all "their" problems. He brought us here to connect with other human beings so that we can walk with others through our collective suffering, clinging together to the Cross of Jesus Christ and the hope of redemption that is offered to us (humanity) in Him alone!

You and I are here to collectively engage in reflecting the unconditional love of Jesus Christ that we have received unto one another and all the people we're here to serve. I am His. He is mine. We are His. He is ours. We have a common suffering and a common hope!

THE PATH OF TRUEST DISCOVERY – HUMILITY

"Yes, I am the vine; you are the branches. Those who remain in Me, and I in them, will produce much fruit. For apart from Me you can do nothing. Anyone who does not remain in Me is thrown away like a useless branch and withers. Such branches are gathered into a pile to be burned. But if you remain in Me and My words remain in you, you may ask for anything you want, and it will be granted! When you produce much fruit, you are My true disciples. This brings great glory to My Father." (John 15:5-8)

I don't know of any other passage in the Bible that assaults my pride more than Jesus saying, "Apart from me you can do nothing." Is that even true? I can do all kinds of things without Jesus!

Where was Jesus when I brushed my teeth this morning? Where was Jesus when I put on my shoes? Of course, that's not what Jesus is talking about in this passage of Scripture. He's saying that without remaining in Him for our source of true life, we cannot produce life's fruit which is fitting for the Master's Table.

The ideas here are very similar to the parable of the sower. Some of the seed fell on good ground produced some fruit. Some of the seed produced a bunch of fruit. Some of the seed produced a ton of fruit. God's desire for us is not that we would merely endure our existence, or even get through life with a few pieces of fruit to show for all the trouble and toil of life.

> **What has been humbling so far on our journey?**

> **Humility is self-perception in divine perspective.**

19

God wants us to bear much fruit! The only way to do that is get a hold of the foundational thought for Christian discipleship – we can't do anything worthy of God for God apart from constant connectedness to Christ. Remaining in Christ means believing that he is God's Son, submitting to Him for who He actually is – Savior and Lord, doing what God says, remaining steadfast in faith in the Good News, and relating in love to the Body of Christ.

Remaining in Christ means daily assaulting our pride with the truth that we can do nothing worthy of Him without Him. Humility is the fruit of a right assessment of me in light of a right assessment of Him.

Week 2: Discovering Christ in our Journey   Day 4

THE PATH OF PURE FRIENDSHIP – HELPFULNESS

"Seek the Kingdom of God above all else, and live righteously, and He will give you everything you need." (Matthew 6:33)

We are at the midpoint of our mission pilgrimage. What have you learned about people? Has anything about true Christian friendship come into your mind, heart, or spirit? By this point on your mission pilgrimage, I'm confident you've at least begun to take in some significant cultural differences.

You may not have had time to process all of it yet, but I bet you've notice the way your missionary guides connect with the indigenous ministry staff, people on the street in the community, and those you've been privileged to serve on our journey.

What has stood out to you? Have you noticed anything different about the willingness of people in this far away land to take joy in meeting your needs? Have you sensed a desire to serve them in return?

What about language barriers? Have you had the profound experience of just connecting on a distinctly human level through eye contact, a smile, a hug, or some other nonverbal means of communication? What about mission team members or the missionaries leading your journey? Have you connected with anyone through service? Is God calling you to go deeper through service?

> **I am most helpful to others when my heart is...**

> **I receive the help of others with joy when...**

> **A weak man with many friends is stronger than even the strongest man on his own.**

When we endeavor to be obedient to God – to live righteously – He will give us everything we need, including fellow pilgrims on our sojourn through the dusty trails of life. "Two people are better off than one, for they can help each other succeed" (Ecclesiastes 4:9).

Is there any greater gift than a friend to help carry the load? What is God teaching us about helpfulness and friendship right now?

STRENGTH FOR THE JOURNEY

> "As for the rest of you, dear brothers and sisters, never get tired of doing good." (2 Thessalonians 3:13)

There are a lot of ways to get tired of doing good. We grow tired from anxiety. When we fail to trust God completely, trusting in our ability, anxiety creeps up and we get tired of doing good. Trusting in our strength to accomplish God's work will always lead to anxiety and weariness.

Weariness is always the guarantee of over-work. The Christian life is a marathon, not a sprint. What's more, it's a relay race. The need for the work we begin today will very likely outlive us. That's the nature of the world. We don't run this race to win by way of accomplishing everything there is to accomplish. We run this race by way of accomplishing everything that God has for us to accomplish.

The single biggest weariness trap for the missionary pilgrim, in the long run, isn't the cheap mattresses, the tight quarters in mission team housing, or the unfamiliar food. Weariness from apparent failure is the enemy's greatest weapon to keep us from continuing to do good for God as we serve others and lead them to Christ.

"What's the use?!" the Devil says. "So many resources have been poured into this place and look at it! It's still a mess!" Christina and I have heard him whisper that many times. "You're wasting your time!

God hasn't called me to...

God is equipping me for...

Fatigue is the fertile soil where Satan sows the seed of doubt.

You're tired. Just give up!" No! I'm running this race to win! What does it mean to win? It means to do all that God has given me to do. He didn't call me to solve all the world's problems. He calls us to obey! He didn't call you to figure out how to "fix" this place in a week. He is calling us to reflect the love of Jesus! That's it.

He calls us to keep doing it, then keep on doing it some more. He calls us to not grow weary or anxious or disheartened by keeping our eyes only on Him, His love, and His power in His time.

THE REASON WE ENDURE THE HARDSHIP – SOULS!

"That is why I said that you will die in your sins; for unless you believe that I AM who I claim to be, you will die in your sins." (John 8:24)

Every day countless souls perish in eternal separation from the love of God because of the rebellion and sedition of the sinful human condition. It's not just that we are a part of a sinful race. You and I are actually, really sinful!

If left to our own devices, who among us would choose sacrifice over pleasure? Without the prevenient grace of God making us aware of our need for Christ, without the preaching of God's Word convicting sinners, who among us would choose to die to self?!

"No one is truly wise; no one is seeking God. All have turned away; all have become useless. No one does good, not a single one." (Romans 3:11-12)

Our task this week has been to be a blessing to people. We've shared the compassion of Christ as we should. We've shared the love of God as we should. But nothing – nothing – is more pressing and of greater concern than being the voice of God's offer in Christ to save sinners from condemnation. The stakes are high! The decisions we make concerning Christ are of eternal consequence. "Whoever has the

> I am the Great Commission.
>
> God saves people through me.
>
> Through us, Jesus shakes a thousand mountains and He awakens countless souls to new life!

Son has life; whoever does not have God's Son does not have life" (1 John 5:12).

Every cup of cold water we share is an opportunity to share the living water of Jesus Christ. Every piece of bread given in Christ's name is an opportunity to speak the Word of Truth and share the Bread of Life.

Make no mistake; the greatest compassion that can be shared is the news that there is hope beyond this life through faith in Jesus Christ! "So if the Son sets you free, you are truly free" (John 8:36).

Strength for the Journey

"You must have the same attitude that Christ Jesus had. Though He was God, He did not think of equality with God as something to cling to. Instead, He gave up His divine privileges; He took the humble position of a slave and was born as a human being. When He appeared in human form, He humbled Himself in obedience to God and died a criminal's death on a cross." (Philippians 2:5-8)

> **A memory to hang on to.**

What a week! The journey affects people differently but it affects everyone. Some people realize that they need to be on a mission more than the people they served need them. They benefit more from the service than the people they serve ever could.

In giving away Christ, they find the purest expression and meaning of what Jesus said in Matthew 10:39, "If you cling to your life, you will lose it; but if you give up your life for Me, you will find it." This is a common consequence.

Other people fall so deeply in love with the people they've met that they know they'll be back. The pilgrimage opens up our hearts in ways we didn't expect or simply couldn't have predicted. God is funny that way. He always has surprises in store!

On a mission pilgrimage, people's faith is strengthened, our assumptions are challenged, are comforts are assaulted, and if we are sensitive to the leading of the Holy Spirit, we are changed. That's a good thing.

> **Memories of God's work in us are fuel for daily endurance.**

What I don't want to happen is that we go back to life as usual and just kind of let the memories of God at work in us slip away or slide out of importance as we return to the normal things of our lives. Take some time to jot down a few memories that, when recalled or talked about, will help us to remember and share what God did in and through us to other people.

Remember, the Christian life is a pilgrimage. It is strapping on our sandals, picking up our walking stick, and following after the Master of Mercy – Jesus Christ!

Week 3: Life as a Third Way Pilgrim

For me, it's the coming back home that is always the hardest. After my first mission trip in Haiti, for example, I remember feeling completely disoriented upon returning to my life in America. It was like being in a dream.

Since that time, I have spoken to a number of missionaries, short term mission team members, and just a ton of people who traveled as pilgrims doing the work of God around the world. This is a normal feeling. It's normal to feel somewhat disoriented upon returning after such a profound experience as well as just getting out of your normal routines, patterns, and experience of the world.

This is a good thing! It means that you experienced something. It means that you got off the couch and carried your cross. What I want to encourage you to do now is to continue to carry a cross every day. Jesus has called us to be pilgrims in this world.

It isn't enough to identify with conservative ideology. It isn't enough to identify with compassion. The life of the Pilgrim follower of Jesus Christ has little to do with being conservative or liberal. It has nothing to do with all the arbitrary categories and boxes within which the world around us wants to make each one of us be identified. You and I are sons and daughters of the King of glory!

You and I have the power within us because of the Holy Spirit to live lives that are distinctly Christian. Today and every day, pick up your walking stick, strap on your sandals, and follow the Master of Mercy – Jesus Christ! Until the next time that we go on another mission pilgrimage together, I'll be praying for you that God would keep you off the couch. Blessings all over you and your walk with the Lord!

MORE FROM ENERGION PUBLICATIONS

Personal Study

The Jesus Paradigm	David Alan Black	$17.99
The Sacred Journey	Chris Surber	$11.99
Crewed Awakening	Greg May	$19.99
Good Morning, Lord!	Linda Estes	$12.99
Daily Devotions of Ordinary People - Extraordinary God	Jody Neufeld	$19.99

Christian Living

Faith in the Public Square	Robert D. Cornwall	$16.99
Grief: Finding the Candle of Light	Jody Neufeld	$8.99
Life in the Spirit	J. Hamilton Weston	$12.99

Bible Study

Learning and Living Scripture	Lentz/Neufeld	$12.99
Inspiration: Hard Questions, Honest Answers	Alden Thompson	$29.99
Colossians & Philemon	Allan R. Bevere	$12.99
Ephesians: A Participatory Study Guide	Robert D. Cornwall	$9.99

Theology

The Politics of Witness	Allan R. Bevere	$9.99
Ultimate Allegiance	Robert D. Cornwall	$9.99
From Here to Eternity	Bruce Epperly	$5.99
The Journey to the Undiscovered Country	William Powell Tuck	$9.99
Eschatology: A Participatory Study Guide	Edward W. H. Vick	$9.99
The Adventist's Dilemma	Edward W. H. Vick	$14.99

Ministry

Clergy Table Talk	Kent Ira Groff	$9.99
Thrive	Ruth Fletcher	$14.99
Out of the Office: A Theology of Ministry	Bob Cornwall	$9.99

Generous Quantity Discounts Available

Dealer Inquiries Welcome

Energion Publications — P.O. Box 841

Gonzalez, FL_ 32560

Website: http://energionpubs.com

Phone: (850) 525-3916